TENNESSEE

BY NATHAN SOMMER

BELLWETHER MEDIA • MINNEAPOLIS, MN

Blastoff! Discovery launches a new mission: reading to learn. Filled with facts and features, each book offers you an exciting new world to explore!

BLASTOFF! UNIVERSE

BLASTOFF! Beginners — GRADE K

BLASTOFF! READERS — GRADES 1-3

BLASTOFF! DISCOVERY — GRADE 4

This edition first published in 2022 by Bellwether Media, Inc.

No part of this publication may be reproduced in whole or in part without written permission of the publisher.
For information regarding permission, write to Bellwether Media, Inc., Attention: Permissions Department,
6012 Blue Circle Drive, Minnetonka, MN 55343.

Library of Congress Cataloging-in-Publication Data

Names: Sommer, Nathan, author.
Title: Tennessee / by Nathan Sommer.
Description: Minneapolis, MN : Bellwether Media, Inc., 2022. |
   Series: Blastoff! Discovery: State profiles | Includes bibliographical
   references and index. | Audience: Ages 7-13 | Audience: Grades 4-6 |
   Summary: "Engaging images accompany information about Tennessee.
   The combination of high-interest subject matter and narrative text is
   intended for students in grades 3 through 8"– Provided by publisher.
Identifiers: LCCN 2021020884 (print) | LCCN 2021020885 (ebook) |
   ISBN 9781644873489 (library binding) | ISBN 9781648341915 (ebook)
Subjects: LCSH: Tennessee–Juvenile literature.
Classification: LCC F436.3 .S67 2022 (print) | LCC F436.3 (ebook) |
   DDC 976.8–dc23
LC record available at https://lccn.loc.gov/2021020884
LC ebook record available at https://lccn.loc.gov/2021020885

Editor: Kate Moening   Designer: Jeffrey Kollock

Printed in the United States of America, North Mankato, MN.

TABLE OF CONTENTS

Please
Do Not Touch

POOL ROOM
GRACELAND

A family is visiting Graceland in Memphis, Tennessee. This house was home to Elvis Presley, one of history's most famous musicians. Music notes decorate the steel front gates. Inside, the family marvels at the Jungle Room. Animal-print furniture stands on thick green carpet.

BEALE STREET

CADES COVE

CLINGMANS DOME

RUBY FALLS

MANY VISITORS

Around 650,000 people visit Graceland each year. The White House is the only home with more yearly visitors!

Their favorite stop is the Pool Room. Bold **paisley** cloth covers the walls and ceiling. They can only imagine the parties thrown there! The tour ends in Graceland's museum. It shows off Elvis's clothes and famous pink Cadillac. Graceland is one of Tennessee's many music landmarks. It is only the beginning of what this state has to offer!

Tennessee sits in the eastern United States. The state is long and narrow. At 42,144 square miles (109,152 square kilometers), Tennessee is the 36th-largest state. Kentucky and Virginia lie to the north. North Carolina sits to the east. The Appalachian Mountains mark this border. Georgia, Alabama, and Mississippi make up Tennessee's southern border. The Mississippi River separates Tennessee from Arkansas and Missouri in the west.

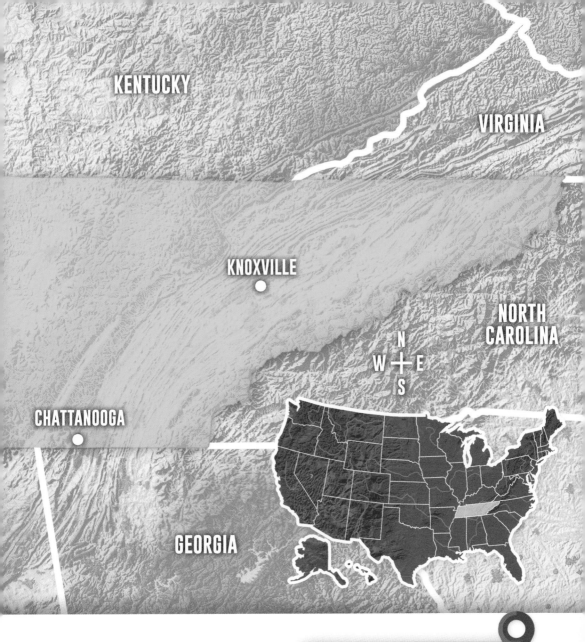

KENTUCKY

VIRGINIA

KNOXVILLE

NORTH CAROLINA

N
W + E
S

CHATTANOOGA

GEORGIA

Nashville is Tennessee's capital and largest city. It is in north-central Tennessee. Memphis is the state's second-largest city. It is in the southwest corner.

THE VOLUNTEER STATE

Tennessee is called the Volunteer State. This is because many Tennesseans have chosen to fight in wars. In the 1840s, about 30,000 Tennesseans volunteered in the Mexican-American War. The government had only asked for 2,800!

TENNESSEE'S BEGINNINGS

FORT LOUDOUN
VONORE

People have lived in Tennessee for more than 12,000 years. Around 900 CE, Mississippian groups built villages and **burial mounds** in the area. They were **ancestors** of the Muscogee, Cherokee, and Chickasaw people.

TENNESSEE AND THE CIVIL WAR

Tennessee fought for the South in the Civil War. But many people in eastern Tennessee did not want to leave the U.S. Tennessee was the last state to leave the United States and the first to rejoin.

In 1540, Spanish explorers arrived in search of gold. French and British explorers came next. They traded fur and land with Cherokee and Chickasaw people. The British built **Fort** Loudoun in 1756. This was one of Tennessee's first European **settlements**. The U.S. took control of the region after the **Revolutionary War**. Tennessee became the 16th state in 1796.

NATIVE PEOPLES OF TENNESSEE

CHEROKEE

- Original lands in central and eastern Tennessee, northern Georgia and Alabama, and western North Carolina
- Descendants largely in the Cherokee Nation of Oklahoma and Qualla Boundary in North Carolina
- Also called Keetoowah, Aniyunwiya, and Tsalagi

CHICKASAW

- Original lands in central and western Tennessee, northern Alabama and Mississippi, and western Kentucky
- Descendants largely in the Chickasaw Nation in Oklahoma

YUCHI

- Original lands in central and eastern Tennessee
- Some descendants now part of the Muscogee Nation in Oklahoma
- Also called Tsoyaha

COUSHATTA

- Original lands in southern Tennessee
- Descendants largely in the Coushatta Tribe of Louisiana
- Also called Koasati

The Appalachian Mountains line Tennessee's eastern border. They include the Blue Ridge and Great Smoky Mountains. Rich river valleys cover the Cumberland **Plateau**. They lead to rolling hills in central Tennessee. The Tennessee River weaves around this region. To the west, the land flattens into grasslands and farms. Forests cover about half of the state.

TENNESSEE RIVER

N
W + E
S

■ CUMBERLAND PLATEAU
■ BLUE RIDGE MOUNTAINS

UNAKA MOUNTAINS
APPALACHIAN MOUNTAINS

CUMBERLAND RIVER
BIG SOUTH FORK NATIONAL RIVER

SEASONAL HIGHS AND LOWS

SPRING
HIGH: 70°F (21°C)
LOW: 48°F (9°C)

SUMMER
HIGH: 88°F (31°C)
LOW: 67°F (19°C)

FALL
HIGH: 71°F (22°C)
LOW: 50°F (10°C)

WINTER
HIGH: 50°F (10°C)
LOW: 31°F (-1°C)

°F = degrees Fahrenheit
°C = degrees Celsius

Tennessee has a **subtropical** climate. Winters are cool and mild. Heavy snowstorms may hit the eastern mountains. Summers are hot and **humid**. The state sees around 50 days of thunderstorms each year. They can lead to dangerous tornadoes.

The Great Smoky Mountains are home to many animals. Deer, spotted skunks, and opossums roam the mountain woodlands. These critters hide from bobcats and coyotes. Black bears also call the woods home. Bats shelter in the area's many caves. They share them with salamanders, lampshade spiders, and wood rats.

Mockingbirds call from Tennessee's trees. Peregrine falcons and great horned owls swoop through the skies. They snatch up cottontails and chipmunks in the meadows of western Tennessee. These birds compete with ground predators such as cottonmouths and rat snakes.

BOBCAT

SPOTTED SKUNK

EASTERN COTTONTAIL

COTTONMOUTH

NORTHERN MOCKINGBIRD

THE CAVE CAPITAL

Tennessee has more than 10,000 caves. It has the most known caves of any state! Thousands of rare fish, bats, and insects live inside these caves.

BIG BROWN BAT

Life Span: up to 20 years
Status: least concern

big brown bat range = ▮

LEAST CONCERN	NEAR THREATENED	VULNERABLE	ENDANGERED	CRITICALLY ENDANGERED	EXTINCT IN THE WILD	EXTINCT
▲						

Nearly 7 million people live in Tennessee. More than one in three Tennesseans live around Nashville and Memphis. The Appalachian Mountain region is more **rural**. Knoxville and Chattanooga are major cities in the area.

TENNESSEE'S FUTURE: HEALTH CARE

Nearly 700,000 Tennesseans do not have health care. They are mostly people of color, young people, and people without jobs. Many cannot afford care. Others do not have clinics nearby. The state needs to lower costs and add clinics to rural regions.

KNOXVILLE

FAMOUS TENNESSEAN

Name: Dolly Parton
Born: January 19, 1946
Hometown: Sevierville, Tennessee
Famous For: One of the best-selling country musicians of all time, she created Dollywood and is part of the Country Music Hall of Fame

Most Tennesseans have European ancestry. Almost one in five Tennesseans are African American or Black. Smaller numbers of Asian American and Native American people also live in Tennessee. More Hispanic Americans are moving to the state. Many recent immigrants came from Mexico. Others are from India, Honduras, and China.

American explorers founded Nashville in 1779. The Cumberland River made it an important trade center. The city has been Tennessee's capital since 1843. Today, Nashville is one of the fastest-growing areas in the U.S. It is home to many universities. It is also a center for finance and health care.

TENNESSEE STATE CAPITOL

ATHENS OF THE SOUTH

Centennial Park has an exact copy of the Parthenon. This famous building stands in Athens, Greece. The park's copy holds the tallest indoor sculpture in the U.S. It is a statue of the Greek goddess Athena!

**PARTHENON
CENTENNIAL PARK**

Nashville offers much to do. Top country musicians perform at the Grand Ole Opry. In the Broadway neighborhood, people go line dancing and hear live music. Locals visit Centennial Park and view art at the Frist Art Museum.

MINING

Farming and railroads fueled Tennessee's early economy. These are still important today. Soybeans and corn are major **exports**. Workers mine for coal in the Cumberland Mountains. In factories, Tennesseans produce computer parts, chemicals, and automobiles. Several major car companies are based in Tennessee.

TENNESSEE'S FUTURE: COLLEGE EDUCATION

Many college students in Tennessee do not finish. These students are often paid less and have fewer job opportunities. Tennessee must better prepare high school students for college. The state can also work to lower college costs and offer students more support.

Service jobs make up most of Tennessee's economy. People work in education and health care. Nashville and the Great Smoky Mountains are tourist centers. There, many people work at hotels, restaurants, and parks. The country music industry creates many jobs in entertainment.

INVENTED IN TENNESSEE

COTTON CANDY

Date Invented: 1897

Inventors: William Morrison and John C. Wharton

SELF-SERVICE GROCERY STORE

Date Invented: 1916

Inventor: Clarence Saunders

TOW TRUCK

Date Invented: 1916

Inventor: Ernest Holmes Sr.

TOUCHSCREEN TECHNOLOGY

Date Invented: 1971

Inventor: Dr. G. Samuel Hurst

DRY RUB RIBS

Barbecue is king in Tennessee kitchens. Memphis barbecue uses a **dry rub** of mixed spices. This seasons pork shoulder or smoked ribs. Nashville is famous for its hot sauce. It is made with cayenne pepper and brown sugar. Tennesseans feel the heat when they eat this spicy sauce on sandwiches and fried chicken!

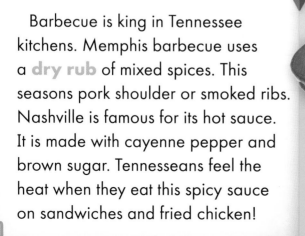

MOON PIE

The Moon Pie is one of Tennessee's proudest inventions. This famous dessert sandwiches marshmallow filling between two graham crackers covered in chocolate!

Catfish from the Tennessee River is another favorite meal. It is often served with fried cornmeal balls called hush puppies. For dessert, Tennesseans enjoy creamy banana pudding topped with crumbled Nilla Wafer cookies. They also love fried apple or blueberry pies!

CATFISH AND HUSH PUPPIES

BANANA PUDDING

NASHVILLE HOT SAUCE

6 SERVINGS

Ask an adult to help you make this spicy recipe!

INGREDIENTS

2 tablespoons cayenne pepper
1 tablespoon brown sugar
1 teaspoon paprika
1 teaspoon salt
1/2 teaspoon black pepper
1/2 teaspoon garlic powder
1/2 cup vegetable oil, heated

DIRECTIONS

1. In a bowl, mix the cayenne pepper, brown sugar, paprika, salt, black pepper, and garlic powder.

2. Add the hot vegetable oil and stir.

3. Using a brush, spread the hot sauce on a sandwich, a piece of chicken, or other food! Stir the hot sauce often as you brush it onto your food.

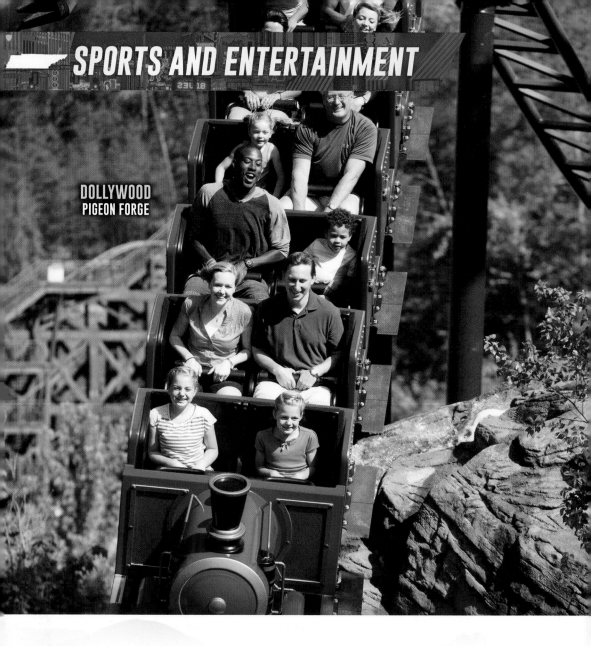

DOLLYWOOD
PIGEON FORGE

There is a lot to do in Tennessee! The Great Smoky Mountains are the most-visited national park in the U.S. People hike, camp, and explore caves. Others raft down rivers for summer fun. In Pigeon Forge, Dollywood offers thrills on roller coasters and water slides. Music fans take in the blues along Beale Street in Memphis. Millions travel to Nashville for world-class line dancing and live country music.

Tennesseans also love sports. Football fans cheer for the Tennessee Titans. The Nashville Predators draw hockey buffs. The Memphis Grizzlies entertain basketball fans. The University of Tennessee's football and women's basketball teams also attract big crowds.

THE LORRAINE MOTEL

The National Civil Rights Museum is in the Lorraine Motel in Memphis. It is the site of Martin Luther King, Jr.'s death. Thousands visit each year to learn about the civil rights movement.

NOTABLE SPORTS TEAM

Tennessee Lady Volunteers
Sport: NCAA Division I women's basketball
Started: 1960
Place of Play: Thompson-Boling Arena

Tennessee offers many festivals.
In June, Lafayette's Hillbilly Days
honors **bluegrass** music and Southern
traditions. Visitors enjoy costume contests,
arts and crafts, and games. Nashville hosts
one of the largest **powwows** east of the
Mississippi River. Each October, the Indian
Education Pow Wow and Arts Exhibition
shows off Native American dances,
drumming, and crafts.

Tennesseans also honor their famous
foods. The Music City Hot Chicken Festival
makes crowds sweat each Fourth of July.
In August, hungry guests visit the Great
Americana BBQ Festival in Franklin. People
eat barbecue from across the country.
Tennesseans love to celebrate their state!

POWWOW
NASHVILLE

BONNAROO MUSIC
AND ARTS FESTIVAL
MANCHESTER

WHICH

BONNAROO

Bonnaroo Music and Arts Festival
is one of the biggest music festivals
in the U.S. Around 80,000 people
travel to Manchester each June.
They experience four days of live
music, camping, tasty food, and more!

1838

The U.S. government forces thousands of Cherokee to leave Tennessee on the Trail of Tears

1540

Explorer Hernando de Soto is the first European to reach what is now Tennessee

1789

Tennessee is split from North Carolina

1796

Tennessee becomes the 16th state

1763

The British take control of Tennessee after winning the French and Indian War

1861

Tennessee leaves the U.S. to join the Confederacy in the Civil War

1934

Great Smoky Mountains
National Park is created

1864

The Union wins the
Battle of Nashville,
the last large battle
of the Civil War

2016

Nashville overtakes
Memphis as
Tennessee's most
populated city

1920

Tennessee is the
36th state to pass the
19th Amendment,
which gives women
the right to vote
nationwide

1968

Civil rights leader
Martin Luther King, Jr.
is killed in Memphis

Nickname: The Volunteer State

Motto: Agriculture and Commerce

Date of Statehood: June 1, 1796 (the 16th state)

Capital City: Nashville ★

Other Major Cities: Memphis, Knoxville, Chattanooga, Clarkesville, Murfreesboro

Area: 42,144 square miles (109,152 square kilometers); Tennessee is the 36th largest state.

Population

6,910,840
(2020)

STATE FLAG

Tennessee's flag has a red background with a blue circle in the middle. Inside the circle are three white stars. These represent the eastern, central, and western parts of the state. A white band surrounds the stars. This represents the state's unity. A wide blue vertical stripe and a thin white stripe line the right edge of the flag.

INDUSTRY

Main Exports

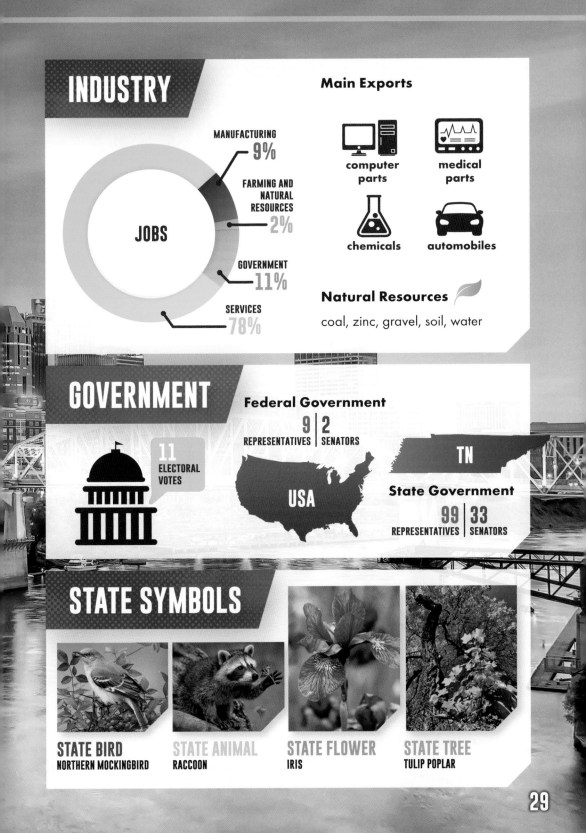

JOBS

- MANUFACTURING **9%**
- FARMING AND NATURAL RESOURCES **2%**
- GOVERNMENT **11%**
- SERVICES **78%**

computer parts

medical parts

chemicals

automobiles

Natural Resources
coal, zinc, gravel, soil, water

GOVERNMENT

Federal Government
9 REPRESENTATIVES | **2** SENATORS

11 ELECTORAL VOTES

USA

TN

State Government
99 REPRESENTATIVES | **33** SENATORS

STATE SYMBOLS

STATE BIRD
NORTHERN MOCKINGBIRD

STATE ANIMAL
RACCOON

STATE FLOWER
IRIS

STATE TREE
TULIP POPLAR

GLOSSARY

ancestors—relatives who lived long ago

bluegrass—a style of music played on string instruments; bluegrass began in the southern Appalachian region of the United States.

buffs—people who are very interested in something and know a lot about it

burial mounds—giant mounds of soil where many prehistoric Native American groups buried their dead

dry rub—a mix of spices that are rubbed onto meat

exports—products sold by one state to another state or region

fort—a strong building where soldiers live

humid—having a lot of moisture in the air

immigrants—people who move to a new country

paisley—a pattern made of curved shapes

plateau—an area of flat, raised land

powwows—Native American gatherings that usually include dancing

Revolutionary War—the war from 1775 to 1783 in which the United States fought for independence from Great Britain

rural—relating to the countryside

service jobs—jobs that perform tasks for people or businesses

settlements—places where newly arrived people live

subtropical—referring to a climate that has hot, humid summers and mild winters

tourist—related to the business of people traveling to visit other places

traditions—customs, ideas, or beliefs handed down from one generation to the next

TO LEARN MORE

AT THE LIBRARY

Perritano, John. *Great Smoky Mountains*. New York, N.Y.: AV2 by Weigl, 2019.

Tieck, Sarah. *Tennessee*. Minneapolis, Minn.: Big Buddy Books, 2020.

Whiting, Jim. *The Story of the Tennessee Titans*. Mankato, Minn.: Creative Education, 2020.

ON THE WEB

FACTSURFER

Factsurfer.com gives you a safe, fun way to find more information.

1. Go to www.factsurfer.com.

2. Enter "Tennessee" into the search box and click 🔍.

3. Select your book cover to see a list of related content.

INDEX